TARANGINI

2

Swami Chinmayananda

and

Swamini Saradapriyananda

CENTRAL CHINMAYA MISSION TRUST

Total no. of copies printed between 1991-2005 - 26000 copies
Revised Edition December 2009 - 5000 copies
Reprint April 2013 - 3000 copies

Published by:
CENTRAL CHINMAYA MISSION TRUST
Sandeepany Sadhanalaya
Saki Vihar Road
Mumbai - 400 072 INDIA
Tel: 91-22-28572367 Fax: 91-22-28573065
Email: ccmtpublications@chinmayamission.com
Website: www.chinmayamission.com

Distribution Centre in USA:
CHINMAYA MISSION WEST
Publications Division
560 Bridgetown Pike
Langhorne PA 19053 USA
Tel: (215) 396-0390 Fax: (215) 396-9710
Email: publications@chinmayamission.org
Website: www.chinmayapublications.org

Design and Illustrations: Nina Bahl

Printed by: Usha Multigraphs Pvt. Ltd., Mumbai 400 013. Tel:- 24925354

Price: ₹ 130/-

ISBN: 978-81-7597-466-1

CTP

CONTENTS

Listen!
Ye Children
of
Immortal Bliss!

Emperor Dileepa

Emperor Dileepa was a great king in the line of the ancestors of Sri Rama. He was young, handsome, good and dedicated to the Lord. He ruled the kingdom justly and powerfully. His wife was called Sudakshina, and in every way was suited to him. Everything was perfect, except that they had no children.

Years rolled by. The king and queen decided to seek the blessings of their Kula Guru, Sage Vashishtha. The king entrusted the administration of the kingdom to his ministers and accompanied by his wife, left in his chariot to meet his Guru in the forest.

They reached the ashrama at sundown and were welcomed by the inmates. They prostrated before their Guru, who blessed them and enquired after the reason for their coming. Dileepa opened up his heart to Vashishtha, revealing that they were unhappy because they had no children. What should they do?

Sage Vashishtha closed his eyes and saw in his divine vision the cause of the queen's childlessness. After a while he opened his eyes and said, "O Dileepa, there is a reason for this condition of yours. Long ago, when you went to the heavens to help Indra in his war with the demons, you were successful. While you were returning to your kingdom in Indra's chariot, passing through Nandanavana, the divine cow Kamadhenu was standing under a Parijata tree. You did not see her as you were preoccupied with thoughts of your wife. In that state of mind, you failed to notice Kamadhenu and pay your respects to her. She felt neglected and cursed you, that you will not have any children until you faithfully worship her child. This curse is the cause for your not having children.

Now do not worry. Nandini, the child of Kamadhenu, is in my ashram. Both of you stay here in tapascharya and serve the cow with full faith and devotion. Let your wife serve her in the ashram. You accompany her when she goes to graze in the forest and carefully protect her. Do this until Nandini is pleased with you. Then she will bless you with children.

The royal couple was extremely glad to know the cause of their childless condition. They prostrated before the sage and took leave of him. Living in the hut allotted to them, they discarded their royal clothes and like the other ashramites wore the bark of trees. They slept in the cowshed along with Nandini, taking care of her at night too. Early every morning Sudakshina cleaned the shed, fed Nandini and milked her.

When she was ready to go for grazing, the king accompanied her, armed with his bow and arrow. The queen accompanied them up to the ashram gate and returned. In the forest the king followed Nandini like a shadow, and did not lose sight of her even for a minute.

7

Thus a fortnight passed. One day the king accompanied Nandini to the forest as usual. He followed her carefully, but somehow in one split-second, when he was not looking, she dodged him and vanished. Where could she be? The king searched for her everywhere anxiously, but could not find her. Suddenly he heard the roar of a lion and the piteous cry of Nandini. He ran in the direction of the sound.

There, in a thick cluster of trees, under a Kadamba tree, he found them both. A fierce-looking lion was attacking Nandini, who lay helplessly on the ground, one paw of the

lion on her heart. Nandini looked at him tearfully and the king blamed himself for his negligence. How could he have been so careless? He must somehow protect her. Immediately he took up his bow and reached for an arrow.

Mysteriously, he found himself paralysed. Neither his hands nor legs could move. He could not draw the bowstring and his hand remained hanging in mid-air. Then the lion spoke in a human voice, "It is futile to fight with me, Dileepa. Do not consider me an ordinary lion. I am the divine vehicle of Parvathi, who loves

this Kadamba tree very dearly. As the wild animals were coming and rubbing their bodies against the trunk of this tree, it was getting spoiled. So Mother ordered me to keep watch to prevent the animals from coming here. All the animals who come here are my prey. Today Nandini has wandered here to become my food. You cannot help her. So go back and allow me to eat her."

Dileepa was helpless. He couldn't move a muscle. How was he to protect his charge? He had only one alternative. He replied gently, "My salutations to you, O divine lion of Mother Parvathi! What you say must be true because I am strangely paralysed, though I am not ill. Nothing is hidden from you as you are divine. Nandini is under my protection and, as a king, it is my duty to protect all who are in danger.

Now that you are determined to kill her, and I am not in a position to protect her with my valour, I am helpless. But if I do not do my duty I shall be blamed. So accept me as your prey and let Nandini go. She will go back to my Guru, who will be waiting for her. Please do me this favour."

The lion agreed to this and released Nandini. Dileepa closed his eyes, ready to be torn to pieces by the lion. And then, a miracle happened. A sweet voice reached his ears, "I am pleased with you, Dileepa. Please open your eyes." Dileepa opened his eyes in surprise. There, before him, stood Nandini.

There was neither the lion nor the cluster of trees. To the wonderstruck king, Nandini spoke, "Do not be surprised. All that happened was an illusion created by me to test you. No one can attack me. I am happy with your dedication. Your tapas is over. You will soon have a son. Let us go back to the ashrama."

The king was overjoyed. He bowed to Nandini with great devotion and they returned to the ashrama. In due course, the king and queen were blessed with a healthy son.

Shravanakumara

Long long ago, there was a boy called Shravanakumara, who dwelt in a forest with his parents. He loved and revered his parents who were old and blind. He looked after their comfort and served them with great love. Whenever they had to go anywhere, he would carefully place them in two baskets and carry them by tying the baskets to the two ends of a strong pole. He would balance the pole on his shoulders and carry them. His parents considered themselves very lucky to have such a devoted son; else, what would have become of them?

One day, Shravanakumara carried them to a forest near Ayodhya. He built a small hut for their stay. At night, he found there was no drinking water in the pot. As his parents were thirsty, he told them that he would go quickly and fetch water from the river. In the darkness he ran to the river with the pot in hand. As he immersed the pot in the river, the water filling the pot made a gurgling sound. Exactly at that time, Dasharatha, the king of Ayodhya, came to the forest to hunt. He was skilled in the art of shooting an arrow in darkness, in the direction of any sound. In this manner, he was able to hunt wild animals that prowled at night.

When Shravanakumara was filling his pot, Dasharatha was on the other side of the river. He heard the sound of the water filling the pot and mistook it for an animal drinking water. So, aiming in the direction of the sound, he shot an arrow. He had very good aim, and the arrow struck Shravanakumara right in the chest. The poor boy fell back with a cry, "Alas! I have been shot. What will happen to my parents now?"

Dasharatha was horrified when he heard the cry. He realised that he had made a terrible mistake and that a human being had been hurt. He came running to the boy's side and found, to his dismay, a brahmin boy writhing in agony, covered in blood. Even in that painful condition, his only thought was for his parents, who were thirsty and waiting for water. Dasharatha approached the boy and explained

to him how he had shot the arrow, mistaking him for a wild animal. He begged his forgiveness.

Shravanakumara cried out, "Oh King! I do not mind dying. But who will look after my blind old parents now? I am all they have. I had come here to fill water for them as they were thirsty. They will be waiting for me. Please carry this water to them and satisfy their thirst. Give them my last pranamas." So saying, Shravana-kumara breathed his last.

Dasharatha was aghast at what he had done. It was not merely one young man whom he had harmed, but also the old parents who would be helpless thereafter. What a terrible thing he had done! All this had happened because of his vicious passion for hunting, and that too in the dark. With a heavy heart, he had to take the drinking water to Shravana's thirsty parents and also inform them of the death of their son.

He took the pot of water and slowly reached the hut. The parents were anxiously waiting for their son, for it was a long time since he had been gone. Had anything happened to him? Such were their thoughts when they heard approaching footsteps. They were happy for they thought that it was Shravanakumara returning. Dasharatha approached them and silently handed over the pot. As they drank the water, he stood nearby to give them the heart-rending news of their son's death.

They finished drinking and asked, "Son, why are you so late?" Then the king spoke, "I am not your son. My name is Dasharatha. I am the king of Ayodhya."

Surprised, they cried out, "Where is our son? Why hasn't he come? How did you come to know of us?"

With great regret, Dasharatha told them how he had mistakenly shot the arrow that killed Sravanakumara. As they listened, the old parents' hearts nearly broke and they bewailed their loss. They asked the king to lead them to the place where their dear son was lying. There they embraced Shravanakumara's body and called his name again and again. What was the use? Their dear, loving boy was no more. At last, they asked the king to arrange a funeral pyre for their boy and for themselves too. They did not want to survive their son.

Shedding remorseful tears, Dasharatha arranged the pyre. They sat on it with the body of their son and told Dasharatha to light it. As they sat there weeping, they cursed Dasharatha, "Oh king, you are responsible for our sorrow. May you also die like us one day, grieving over the separation from your son."

The curse had its effect long afterwards, when Sri Rama went to the forest. Dasharatha died, pining for a glimpse of his beloved son.

17

Srikalahasti

Once upon a time there was a tiny spider. It was very devoted to Lord Shiva. One day, while in a forest, the spider found a Linga and was irresistibly drawn toward it. From that day onwards, the spider remained there to serve the Lord. Every day, the spider would move around the Linga and weave webs of beautiful patterns to decorate the Lord. This went on for a number of years. At last the Lord, pleased with this devotion, decided to test the spider. One day, the spider cleaned up the previous day's web and began weaving a new one. The Lord waited till the pattern was almost complete. Then he opened his third eye a little. The whole web, beautifully woven for hours, was burnt in a second.

The poor spider was very sad. It again started weaving a fresh pattern to serve as a canopy for the Lord. The Lord again waited until the web was completed, and once more opened his third eye. The pattern was reduced to ashes in no time, the labour of the spider having been wasted again. But the spider was not dispirited. It commenced once again; but the same fate awaited the third web too. Thus it happened many times and the spider was at its wits end. It did not know how to provide a permanent shelter for its beloved Lord. As the tenth pattern was burning, the spider jumped into the fire in despair and immolated itself. The Lord, happy with its devotion, liberated it.

The Linga continued to remain there. One day a snake saw the Linga and became devoted to the Lord. Full of devotion, it would come to the Linga every day and offer worship with valuable gems of the snake world, prostrate, and take leave for the day. At about the same time, an elephant walking in the forest also saw the Linga and became attached to it. The elephant too picked up the habit of visiting the Linga every day. Sprinkling it with water with his trunk, he would offer flowers and leaves plucked from the trees, and leave for the day.

Both the snake and the elephant thus became regular devotees, without actually meeting. Each knew of the puja of the other. The elephant saw the costly gems, but did not know their value. So it would push the useless stones aside contemptuously, and offer flowers instead. The snake did not understand the freshness of the

flowers. In utter contempt, it would push away the flowers and offer the gems. This went on for some time until gradually they developed a hatred for each other and became bitter enemies.

One day the snake was determined to find out who the heartless creature was who removed his loving offerings. So, that day, instead of clearing the floral offerings to offer its own seva, it lay hidden within the heap of flowers to see who came to worship the Lord. The elephant came at its usual time. When it saw its offerings intact, it felt happy thinking that its rival had not come for puja.

Thinking that the Lord had accepted its offering and not that of its rival, it stretched out its trunk to clear the previous day's flowers. Immediately, the snake hidden in the flowers entered its trunk. It crawled up and stayed coiled up in the elephant's brain. The poor elephant was in great pain. It ran hither and thither, moving its trunk in every direction, trumpeting piteously, but whatever it did, it could not touch the snake, which was smugly seated in its brain.

The elephant cried out to the Lord. At last, unable to bear the pain any longer, it dashed headlong against the Linga. The violence of the impact crushed both the elephant's head and the snake inside it, killing them both. The Lord, pleased with their devotion, gave them Liberation.

In order that people would remember the inspiring sacrifices and pure devotion of these dumb creatures, the Lord took on their shapes. The place where the spider, the elephant and the snake attained moksha came to be called Srikalahasti. The Lord here is known as Srikalahastiswara, the Lord of Sri, Kala and Hasti or the spider, snake and elephant, respectively.

The Linga has the three signs of the three devotees — a spider's web, the elephant's tusk, and the coiled snake, which can be seen even today.

22

Helpers in Eating

Once a man and his wife came to the durbara of a king who was very, very kind and considerate to his people. Anyone in need could approach him and seek his help. When the couple came to the court, the king asked them what they needed. The couple said that they were very poor and did not have any property. They prayed for some means of livelihood.

The king ordered that they be given two buffaloes so that they could sell the milk and earn money. The couple was overjoyed. They went home happily singing the king's praises.

A week later, the couple was back in the king's court. The king kindly asked them what they needed. The couple said that it was getting very difficult for them to go to the market and sell the milk. They prayed for some help in selling the milk in the market. The king ordered one of his cowherds to go to their house daily, collect the milk, sell it in the market and give the money to them. The happy couple returned home joyfully praising the king.

Again, a week later, the husband and wife returned to the king's court. The king asked them what they wanted. They sadly said that the buffaloes needed a lot of care and that it was difficult to milk them. They would be very grateful if someone could be deputed to help them in this task.

The king ordered one of his cowherds to go to their house daily, attend to the buffaloes and milk them. The couple was overjoyed. Praising the king, they left.

Another week passed and the couple was in the court again. When the king asked them what they required this time, they said with a sorrowful expression, that it was very, very difficult for them to cook their food every day. They would be ever grateful to the king if he could provide them with a cook. The king told them not to worry; he would send one of his cooks to do their kitchen work. They were besides themselves with joy. Thanking and praising the king profusely, they left.

The next morning the king's cook arrived at the couple's house. The wife showed him the kitchen and the stores and gave instructions about preparing the food. She told him that they wanted their meal exactly at twelve o'clock. The cook nodded his head in assent.

At twelve o'clock they got up from their beds and went to the dining room to have their lunch. The table was laid neatly with two plates. The cook was ready with the meal. Satisfied that everything was according to their orders, the husband and wife went to the tap, washed their hands and returned. As they reached the dining table, two hefty-looking people, a man and a woman, came out of the kitchen, sat down at the table and started eating. The cook served them carefully and courteously, and they finished all the delicious dishes one by one before their very eyes! The couple ran to the table in consternation and asked, "Who are you? Why are you eating our food?"

They lifted their heads and replied with a smile, "The king sent us to help you in eating.

You don't have to bother at all about eating. From now on we will eat for you. You needn't bother yourselves at all. Please go and rest."

The husband and wife ran to the court and prayed to the king, "O kind King! Please withdraw all the help from our house. From now on we will gladly do all our chores by ourselves." Smiling broadly, the king nodded in assent.

The Robber Guru

Once there was an old couple who lived in a village. They had no children and lived all by themselves. They were pious and simple and had a good word for everyone. One day, they heard that a Guru was needed in order to gain Liberation. So they thought that they must immediately find a Guru, else they might die without being initiated. As there were no Gurus in their village, they locked up their house and set out in search of one.

While passing through a forest, they met a white-clothed sadhu whose forehead was smeared with sandal-paste and who wore a tulasi mala around his neck. From his dress they understood that he must be a great devotee of Lord Vishnu and he appeared as though he could give them initiation.

So, falling at his feet, they begged him to accept them as his disciples and give them a mantra. Actually, the man was not a sadhu at all but a robber who had committed a theft. He was escaping from the police in the guise of a sadhu. When the old couple fell at his feet, he tried to free himself, so that he could escape quickly as the police were in hot pursuit. But the old couple did not leave him.

Now the robber was in a fix. He did not know how to get rid of them. He thought the best way was to give them some instructions and quickly make his escape. So he smiled and said, "Get up, my children. I was merely testing whether you were sincere devotees or not. Now that I am convinced of your sincerity, I shall give you instructions."

The couple was very happy and stood up. The robber told them that they should stand with one leg bent in front and the other stretched behind. They did so. "Now close your eyes and join your palms in salutation," he said. They did as they were told. "Now repeat the Lord's name, Narayana, Narayana..." They started repeating the name. "Good," the robber Guru instructed, "continue to stand in this posture and repeat the name continuously until the Lord comes and gives you darshana. Meanwhile, don't open your eyes." They

nodded without opening their eyes, repeating the mantra. The robber thanked his stars at their gullibility and quickly escaped.

Two or three days passed. Following the instructions of their Guru, the old couple stood in the same posture without the least movement, fervently repeating the mantra given to them. Innocent and ignorant as they were, their fervour was great. Their tapas

heated up the heavens and disturbed Narayana, who was lying on his snake-bed. When He saw the determination of the old couple, He came down along with Lakshmi to give them darshana. Standing before the couple, He called out, "O devotees, I am pleased with your tapas. I have come to give you darshana. Open your eyes."

The couple opened their eyes and immediately closed them again. Surprised, the Lord asked, "Why have you closed your eyes again? I have come to give you boons!"

The couple said, "Sir, our Guru told us only about Narayana. He did not tell us that Narayana would come with a lady. How can we be sure that you are really Narayana and not someone else come to deceive us? We will wait until the Lord comes to us as told by our Guru."

How innocent they were! They had implicit faith in their Guru. So Lakshmi and Narayana disappeared. Narayana then took the form of the robber Guru and spoke. "Children, open your eyes. I am your Guru who has come to give you some more instructions."

Hearing their Guru's voice, they opened their eyes and prostrated. They said, "O Teacher, as we were repeating the name of the Lord, someone came with a lady and declared to us that he was Narayana. We did not believe him as you did not tell us about the lady."

The Guru smiled kindly and said, "Yes, I know, my children. That is why I have come again. Narayana is married. It was His wife Lakshmi who came along with Him. Next time when both of them come, prostrate before the Lord and ask for boons." He blessed them and disappeared. They were relieved to get their Guru's assurance. This time, when Lakshmi and Vishnu appeared together and called out as before, the couple prostrated to them and sought moksha. The Lord blessed them and granted them the boon of Liberation.

The Sweetness of Devotion

 When the Pandavas completed their twelve years of dwelling in the forest and one year without being recognised, they wanted to get their kingdom back from the Kauravas. Sri Krishna came to Hastinapura as their ambassador to hold talks with Duryodhana and his brothers.

In Hastinapura, Sri Krishna was invited both by Duryodhana and Vidura to eat with them. Though Vidura was poor and could not offer royal meals like Duryodhana, Sri Krishna accepted Vidura's invitation because he was a great devotee. At lunch time, Vidura took Sri Krishna home with great reverence and Vidura's wife, who was even more devoted than her husband, rushed forward to receive the Lord. She prostrated before Him and garlanded Him.

With great love, the husband and wife served food to the Lord. The Lord loved the food though it was simple, because He knew how much the couple loved Him. After the meal Vidura's wife brought nice ripe plantains for Sri Krishna. In the presence of the Lord she forgot herself, her house, husband and even what she was doing. Gazing at the sweet face of the Lord, she picked up the plantains one by one, peeled them and put the skin into His mouth.

The Lord too, forgot Himself. He was

lost in the devotion of the woman and ate whatever she fed Him. The plate was almost empty, when suddenly, Vidura came into the room. To his horror, he found that his wife was unconsciously throwing away the fruit and putting the skin into Sri Krishna's mouth. In great consternation, he cried out to his wife, "You fool! What have you done? You have fed the Lord with plantain skins!"

The ecstasy of Vidura's wife was broken by this cry from her husband. Looking down, she saw what she had done. Shedding tears of remorse, she picked up the fruit carefully and tried to put it into the mouth of the Lord. The ecstasy of the Lord also was broken and He did not like the taste of the fruit. He said, "No more, please. This is not as sweet as what you gave me before!"

Is there any difference for the Lord between the skin and the fruit? Both are created by Him. What He tastes is the sweetness of our devotion when we offer something to Him.

In the City of the Stupid King

Once there lived a king called Pancha Maha Pataka, that is, one who has committed five great sins. As he was not very clever, he did not think clearly, and his judgement was poor. Evil and injustice triumphed in his kingdom and the good and the innocent suffered due to the king's dim understanding. The people mutely prayed to the Lord for deliverance from this tyrant. Deliverance came to them, and that too, suddenly and miraculously, in the most unexpected manner.

There was a rich merchant in the kingdom, who was having his house repaired. One night, two thieves broke into his house. As they were crawling through a hole, the wall which was still wet, collapsed killing one of the thieves on the spot. The other thief ran away, but he was very angry with the merchant and burned to avenge his friend's death.

The next morning he rushed to the king's court with a complaint against the merchant for having caused his friend's death by putting up a wet mud wall. The foolish king, with his perverted reasoning, could not understand who was in the wrong. He flew into a rage with the merchant when he heard the thief's complaint. An eye for an eye and a tooth for a tooth was the only law he knew.

He immediately sent for the merchant and asked him sternly, "Oh merchant! Why did you put up a wet wall instead of a dry one? Your negligence has caused the death of the poor thief, who innocently broke into your house." The stunned merchant stood helplessly, not knowing how to reply to this unreasonable allegation. Unless he said something that was acceptable to the king, he would surely be hung on the scaffold. Thinking desperately, he suddenly came up with an answer.

"O King! You know that I hired a mason to build the wall. I told him to put up a dry wall. He disobeyed my instructions and put up a wet wall. The fault therefore is his, not mine."

"Is that so?" said the king. "Then you are not responsible. You may go now. I shall punish the mason." The mason was sent for, and he came, trembling with fear.

The king shouted at the mason, "You fool! When the merchant told you to put up a dry wall, why did you put up a wet wall? Because of your mistake the innocent thief died. You shall pay for it with your life." The poor mason was at a loss. The king did not even know that dry walls could not be put up. How could he escape his wrath? Bowing low to the king he said, "O King, this was what I instructed the labourer to do. He mixed too much water in the mud and so the wall became wet. It was not my mistake, as you can see."

"Is that so?" thundered the king. The labourer was sent for and he too, came trembling.

"Why did you pour too much water in the mud? Because of your mistake, the wall was wet and the innocent thief died. Why should I not hang you for it?" asked the king.

The labourer trembled in fright and said, "O King, please listen to me. I did not put too much water. It was the potter's mistake. He made the mouth of the pot too wide because of which more water fell into the mud than I had intended. I am innocent."

"Is that so?" asked the king, "Then I won't punish you. The potter is the culprit, you may go." The labourer ran for his life. The potter was summoned.

"You foolish man! Why did you make the mouth of the pot too wide? Because of you an innocent thief has died. I shall hang you." The potter knew that neither reason nor logic would weigh with the king. Only a silly excuse could help him out of his predicament. He replied, "O King! Please hear me out first. When I was making the pot, a beautiful woman passed by on the road. She was so beautiful that I forgot what I was doing. I gaped at her until she passed out of my sight. At that moment, the mouth of the pot became too wide. Had the woman not walked on the road at that time, this would not have happened."

"Is that so?" roared the king. "In that case you are not guilty. I shall hang the woman." The woman was sent for. The poor woman came, frozen with terror.

"Why did you walk on the road on the day when the potter was making pots?" The mouth of the pot became too wide because the potter gaped at you. An innocent thief died because of you. Why should I not hang you?" The woman looked tearfully at the king and said, "O King, would I be walking on the road just for fun? I gave an order to the goldsmith long ago to make an ornament for me. He had been delaying it for months. Therefore, I had to go to his house and remind him. It is his fault, not mine."

"Is that so?" cried the king. "Then the goldsmith must be hung, not you. You may go. I shall deal with the goldsmith."

"Why did you delay the making of the ornament for such a long time? Because you delayed it the woman had to come to your house on that day and the potter gaped at her,

therefore the mouth of the pot became too wide. I shall hang you for it," said the king.

The goldsmith was a shrewd man. He thought for a while and said, "O King, the merchant didn't give me the gold for a long time. That is why the ornament was delayed."

"Is that so?" said the king, "Then you may go. I shall hang the merchant." The merchant was sent for. "Why didn't you give the gold to the goldsmith in time? Because of you, the ornament was delayed and the woman walked on the road and the potter made the mouth of the pot too wide. An innocent thief died falling under the wall. You appear to be the worst of rogues. I shall hang you!"

The poor merchant shrank back in fear. But he could not come up with a silly excuse, like the others and escape. So the king concluded that the merchant was the real culprit and gave him the death sentence. He was to be hanged early the next morning. The sentence of death was proclaimed in the whole kingdom and all the people were asked to be present at the time of the hanging so that it would serve as a warning to all evil-doers.

The proclamation caused a wave of shock and outrage in the people. Everyone felt that it was unjust to punish the merchant. But how were they to save him?

In a forest nearby, there was a small ashrama where a great sage lived with his disciples. Some elders of the kingdom approached the sage and told him how the king had passed a death sentence on an innocent man, and requested him to save the merchant. The sage agreed to do his best.

Early next morning the merchant was brought to the place of hanging, where the noose was ready. All the people had gathered there as ordered. The king and all the officers were present too. Everyone was tense as the merchant was about to be hanged. Suddenly there was a commotion. The sound of voices raised in heated argument rent the air. The king angrily ordered his soldiers to arrest the troublemakers who had disturbed the solemn

45

occasion. The soldiers went into the crowd, found the sage and his disciple and dragged them before the king. Frowning, the king asked the sage, "Why are you creating such a disturbance here?"

The sage said, "O King, I beg your pardon. My disciple picked a quarrel with me. I want to be hanged in place of the merchant, but my disciple wants to get hanged instead. Please allow me to be hanged in place of the merchant."

The disciple came forward and said, "O King, please hang me in place of the merchant. My Guru is very selfish. He wants to get himself hanged and will not allow me to offer myself. This is not fair."

The king was astonished. "Any man in his senses would try to escape hanging. Why do you both want to die?" The sage and his disciple looked at each other. Then the sage turned to the king and said, "King, this is a great secret which I don't want to reveal. Please order the soldiers to release the merchant and hang me instead." "No, please O King, hang me," beseeched the disciple.

"I shall hang neither of you, unless you tell me the reason," the king said.

Feigning great reluctance, the sage said, "O King, whoever gets hanged today will be born as the king of this kingdom in his next life. Please allow me to be hanged."

"Look at my Guru's selfishness. He does not want me to have a chance to become king. Please hang me instead," pleaded the disciple.

When the king heard this, he got very angry. "I am the king of this kingdom. I shall be king in the next life too!" He got up from his chair, walked to the gallows and ordered the soldiers to release the merchant. Then he signalled to the executioner to put the noose round his neck. He was hanged by the neck until he was dead and thus the people were freed from the foolish king, Pancha Maha Pataka.

Kindness Pays

Once upon a time there was a king with two wives. The elder queen was very unhappy because the king seldom paid any attention to her and spent most of his time with the younger queen.

Unable to bear the partiality of the king, the elder queen decided to put an end to her life. One morning she left the palace and walked towards the river. On the way she saw a dried-up plant that was about to die. The plant called out to the queen and said, "Mother, please remove all dried leaves lying around me and clear the passage that brings me water from the canal." The queen had a kind and considerate heart. Feeling sorry for the plant, she went near it and gently shook off all the dried leaves. She cleared the passage from the canal to the plant so that the water flowed freely again. Her work finished, she took leave of the plant and went on her way to the river.

As she walked, she came across a cow, emaciated and feeble, tied in a dirty shed. The cow cried out to her, "Mother, please clean my shed and get me some grass and water. I am starving." The queen felt sorry for the cow. She went into the shed and cleaned it carefully. Then she drew water from the nearby well and filled the tank near the cow. She cut plenty of grass and placed it close to the cow. The work finished, she took leave of the cow and walked on.

When she approached the river she found a Rishi sitting on its bank in a dilapidated hut. She went to the Rishi and prostrated before him. Then she saw that the hut was in a very bad shape. She brought some bamboos and branches and repaired and cleaned the hut. She saw a mud pot in the corner of the hut. She cleaned it and filled it with fresh water. She also saw some flour in a tin. As it was lunch time, she lit a fire and prepared a meal for the Rishi and offered it to him. The Rishi ate the food and blessed her.

As she took leave of him to go to the river, the Rishi, who knew who she was and why she was going to the river, told her, "Mother, just take one dip in the river and come back."

The queen had come to jump into the river and end her life. But how could she disobey the Rishi? She did as he had told her. Lo! When she

emerged from the water after one dip, she found herself transformed into a very young and graceful woman, with long dark tresses that came down to her heels. She was happy beyond words. She returned to the hut and prostrated before the sage once again. Smiling kindly he said, "Mother, do not think of suicide any more. Go back to your palace. The king will love you and look after you very well."

As she was returning joyfully, the cow called out to her. The loving care of the queen had made the cow stronger and full of milk. She told the queen, "Mother, drink my milk. It will do you good." The queen did as she was told. As she drank the milk, she felt refreshed, full of energy and youthful vigour. The cow blessed her, saying that she would always have the same vigour.

She thanked the cow and walked on. When she came to the plant, it called out to her. Now, with all the care bestowed on it by the queen, the plant was in full bloom and the fragrance of its flowers filled the whole area. The plant told her to pluck some flowers and put them in her hair. The queen did as she was told and her whole body became fragrant. The plant blessed her and said that the fragrance would remain with her forever. The queen expressed her gratitude to the plant and started towards the palace. As she walked towards it, the people she met looked at her again and again, wondering at her beauty. When she entered the palace, it became aglow with her splendour and filled with sweet fragrance.

The king wondered where this fragrance came from. When he saw the queen he gaped in wonder at her grace and beauty. He felt attracted towards her and began to spend all his time with her. Her kindness and consideration, her intelligence and calm temperament attracted him more and more. In comparison, the younger queen seemed like a faded flower.

Now the younger queen grew restless with jealousy and anger. She made secret enquiries as to how the elder queen had got her charming beauty. She thought that she too would try to get the blessings of the Rishi and become younger and more beautiful than the elder queen.

The next day, early in the morning, she left the palace and walked towards the river. On the way, a dried-up plant called out to her, "Mother, please shake dry leaves lying around me and clear the passage that brings me water from the canal." The haughty queen frowned and shouted, "Do you think I am your gardener? I am busy. I can't attend to your silly requests."

She walked ahead. On the way, a hungry and emaciated cow in a shed cried out to her, "Mother, please clean my shed and get me grass and water." The proud queen scowled and shouted at the cow. "Do you think that I am a cowherd? I am very busy. I can't attend to your silly requests."

She walked ahead and reached the river. On the banks she saw the dilapidated hut of the sage. She went and prostrated before the Rishi stiffly and said, "Please bless me with the same beauty as the elder queen."

The Rishi smiled and said, "Mother, it is not I that blesses. It is your own goodness that blesses you. Go to the river and take one dip. You will get what you deserve."

The queen went to the river and took one dip. When she arose from the water, alas, she was very ugly and old. Most of her hair had fallen and the remaining had turned white. Horrified, the queen took one more dip and yet another. The more dips she took, the uglier she grew.

Weeping bitterly, she went to the sage and complained that he had cursed her instead of blessing her. The Rishi looked at her kindly and said, "No, Mother, no one can either bless or curse you. It is your own mind that curses or blesses you. You are jealous, proud, haughty and unsympathetic. You look what you are. Repent for all your wrongdoings and live a pure life. Then you will become truly beautiful."

The Rama Thief

The saint of Kanhangada, Papa Ramadasa, during his wanderings throughout the country once happened to go to a town. Nearby there were some hillocks with caves. Papa Ramadasa stayed in one of the caves for a fortnight. Gradually, as people became aware of the presence of a Mahatma, they started visiting him and spending time with him in satsang.

Soon Papa Ramadasa, with his broad smile and talk of Rama, became dear to all. People started bringing him presents. He accepted all with a smile and thanked Rama. Slowly, a cot, bed, clock, tiffin carrier, water bottle and several other articles got collected in the cave. The devotees would spend the whole day in the presence of the saint and leave for their homes in the evening as it became dark. Throughout the night Papa remained alone, lost in contemplation of God.

A thief came to know that the cave was full of valuable things and that during the night the swami was alone without help or even light. He thought it would be easy to rob him.

So one night, after all the devotees had left, the thief entered the cave. Papa Ramadasa was sitting on the bed in deep meditation. The thief focused his torch on him and ordered, "Spread the bedsheet on the floor and put all the things on it." Papa joyously obeyed. He neatly spread the bedsheet on the ground and brought the mattress, the clock and the tiffin carrier, the water bottle and all the other things that were in the cave. The thief carefully checked to see that nothing was left. When he was satisfied, he

ordered Papa to tie the bundle and put it on his back. Papa did so. The thief took up the cot with one hand and the bundle with the other and walked out. There was no protest or outburst from Papa.

Papa sat on the ground and was soon lost in meditation again. Morning came. With it came the devotees, bringing coffee and tiffin for Papa.

When the devotees saw that the whole cave was empty and Papa was sitting on the ground, with his usual smile, they could not imagine what had happened. One of them made bold to ask, "Maharaja, where are all the articles that were here yesterday?"

Papa Ramadasa laughed and said, "Rama took them away."

They were surprised and asked, "Which Rama?"

Papa again laughed and said, "Which Rama? There is only one Rama. Rama gave them and Rama took them away."

Slowly, bit by bit the devotees heard the whole story. When they saw how perfectly happy the saint was without a trace of regret for all that was lost, they marvelled at his detachment and realised how a man could be truly free.

The Three Fish

Once upon a time three fish lived together in a tank. One was called Dirghadarsi, which means one who can think ahead. The second fish was known as Praptakalajna, or one who is a quick thinker. The third one was called Mandabuddhi, or the dull-witted one. The three were friends and lived together happily.

As summer approached, Dirghadarsi saw that the water level was going down. So she told her companions, "As summer advances the water will dry up and the fishermen will easily catch us in their nets. Let us leave this tank and swim to a deeper one." The other two smiled indulgently but showed no signs of accepting her advice. Dirghadarsi then acted on her own. She swam away from the tank alone and went to a deeper tank that was safe to live in.

Gradually, what Dirghadarsi had foretold came to pass. The water became less and less

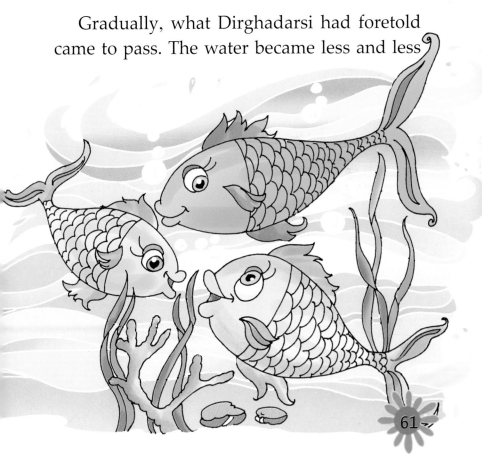

and the fishermen could easily see the fishes swimming across the tank under the water. They cast their nets and the two fish, Praptakalajna and Mandabuddhi were caught.

Praptakalajna did some quick thinking. She lay still, pretending to be dead. The fisherman saw the dead fish. He picked her up and threw her aside. Immediately, the fish jumped back into the tank and found a place of hiding.

Naturally, the foolish Mandabuddhi was very upset at having been caught. She could not think at all. In great anxiety she jumped up and down, trying to escape from the net. But the fisherman noticed her, caught her firmly by the tail and put her in the basket to be taken to the market!

The Three Sons of
the Minister

Once a certain king had a minister who was very intelligent and shrewd. As the minister was growing old and feeble, the king was worried about finding a successor for him. So he asked the minister whether he knew anyone who could succeed him. The old man said, "I have three sons, but they differ greatly from one another in temperament. The first one is a daredevil, the second is a diplomat, and the third is straightforward and honest. You may wish to test and choose one of them."

Intrigued, the king asked the minister to arrange the test. The minister thought for a moment and said, "Sir, please remain in this room. I shall send for my sons one by one and give them identical orders. You may watch how each one acts and then you will know which one to choose."

Accordingly, the minister went into the next room while the king remained where he was. From there he could hear what was being said in the other room.

When his eldest son came, the minister said, "Son, you know the rose garden of the king, don't you?"

The son nodded to indicate that he knew the rose garden. The minister went on, "The king loves the garden so much that he does not permit anyone to pluck the flowers. In the centre of the garden is the 'President' rose, which is a very rare plant. The king has passed an order that anyone plucking its flowers will be put to death."

The son nodded his head again as he was familiar with all these facts. The minister said, "Tomorrow you must go to the garden exactly at ten o' clock in the morning and pluck one 'President' rose for me. Do not allow the guards either to see you or catch you. If they catch you, make use of your mouth and escape."

The son listened to the instructions carefully, agreed to carry them out and took leave of his father.

Next, the second son was sent for and the same instructions were given to him, except that he was asked to go to the garden at twelve noon. The third son was instructed to go at two o' clock in the afternoon.

After the three sons were thus directed, the minister sent for the guards and told them, "Tomorrow, my three sons will come at ten o' clock in the morning, at noon and at two o' clock in the afternoon, to your garden. Do not catch them when they enter. They will go straight to the 'President' rose and pluck one flower. As soon as the flower is plucked, you surround them and bring them here along with proof of their guilt. But don't hurt them in any

manner." The guards understood what was expected of them and went away.

The next day, exactly at ten in the morning, the eldest son entered the garden. All the guards had hidden themselves and were watching. The minister's son congratulated himself on not being seen by anyone. He went to the 'President' rose and plucked one flower, and was immediately surrounded by the guards. He remembered his father's instructions, that he should escape by using his mouth. He was a hefty young man, endowed

with strong teeth and a powerful voice, and he roared and thundered and bit the guards who winced in pain. He escaped and they could do nothing but report what had happened to the king.

When the second son plucked the flower at noon, the guards surrounded him but were careful to keep him at a distance lest he too should bite them. The second son did nothing of the sort. The guards could keep him in their midst and march him to the palace. As they were marching, the minister's son, remembering his father's instructions that he should use his mouth and escape, opened his mouth and quickly swallowed the rose. By the time the guards tried to stop him it was too late. Now what was the use of taking him to the king without the proof? So the guards let him go and reported to the king what had happened.

The third son also was caught in the same manner. He made no attempt either to hurt the guards nor did he swallow the flower. He came to the presence of the king along with the flower. When the guards reported the matter to the king, the king looked sternly at him and asked, "Have you no desire to live? Why did you disobey my order?"

The youth bowed and said, "Sir, before you punish me, please allow me to explain the matter. Yesterday, my father, the minister called me into this very room and instructed me to pluck the flower. Since it was the order of the minister, there must be some important reason for it. My father can explain this. Then punish me if you think it necessary."

The king, of course, released the minister's son. He thought over the incidents, wondering how three sons born to the same parents could differ so widely in temperament. He understood that all beings are born with their own tendencies and will always behave differently.

Taking their different temperaments into consideration, the king selected the first son as chief of the army, the second son as chief minister and the third as his chief adviser.

The Greedy Master

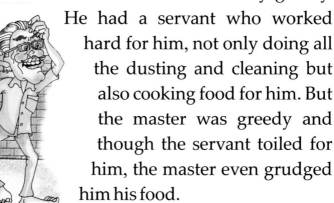

Once there was a man who was very greedy. He had a servant who worked hard for him, not only doing all the dusting and cleaning but also cooking food for him. But the master was greedy and though the servant toiled for him, the master even grudged him his food.

One day, the servant cooked a dainty delicacy. The dish looked very tempting and the greedy master wanted to eat the whole thing himself, without sharing it with the servant. But on what pretext could he do so? He thought of a plan. He told the servant, "Let us not eat the dish now. We will go to sleep now, and whoever has the best dream will eat it all." The servant had no choice but to agree.

Both master and servant slept for a few hours. When they got up, the master called the servant and said, "I had the most wonderful dream. I dreamt that I was the emperor of the whole of India. I had a palace with thousands and thousands of servants. My harem was full of ladies who were as beautiful as the heavenly nymphs. I was being served by them. But then I woke up. I still feel as if I am there. This was my dream. What was your dream?" He was sure that the ignorant servant could not conjure up a better dream than his. He would have to accept defeat and leave the full dish for his master.

The servant was not educated, but he was quick-witted. He had understood his master's trick when it was proposed. So he had calmly eaten the dish while his master was sleeping and thought out what he would say when the master asked him about his dream. So he said with a gloomy face, "O Master, I was not as lucky as you. I had a terrible dream. The moment I went to sleep a terrifying demon appeared and started beating me. I cried out in pain and begged for mercy. Then he stopped and said that he would spare me if I went into the kitchen and ate the entire dish; otherwise, he threatened to kill me there and then. Frightened out of my wits, I rushed into the kitchen."

"And then what did you do?" the master asked anxiously. "What could I do, Sir? I ate up the whole thing. The demon was standing right behind me with the lathi in hand, ready to knock my head off, if I left anything in the dish."

The master ran into the kitchen to see for himself. There, in front of him, was the dish — all empty and cleaned out. Just near the dish was a huge lathi supposedly used by the demon to frighten the servant. The master smarted under his disappointment. Had he shared the dish with his servant, he could have at least tasted it. By trying to be too clever he did not even get a whiff of it!

The Eyes that Sin

Suradasa was a great devotee of Lord Krishna. He was blind and could not see the gross world, but the fervour of his devotion opened his inner eye and he could visualise Krishna, the Blue Boy of Vrindavan, in his mind. Out of his sweet love for the Lord, the story of Krishna flowed through his voice in a melody of poetry known as *Surasagara*. It is said that when he sang the *Surasagara*, Bhagavan Krishna used to come and sit in front of him like a small boy and enjoy the poetry.

This great devotee was content with life. He had no desire at all for anything in the world.

But sometimes he felt sad at his blindness. If he had his eyes, he would have gone to Vrindavan to see all those sacred places where his Lord spent His childhood, playing mischievous pranks with the gopis and gopas of Vrindavan. Sri Krishna knew his desire, blessed him and granted him the much longed-for eyesight.

Suradasa was overjoyed. He immediately set out for Vrindavan. He saw the various places connected with the Lord's childhood, touched them all with devotion, prostrated before them with great fervour and filled with gratitude, every minute praised the Lord who had restored his eyesight. Then he came to a famous temple of Krishna and wanted to enter it. The pujari had just finished his morning duty and was about to lock the temple. Suradasa requested him to allow him to have darshana of the Lord. The pujari had no inkling who Suradasa was, and told him to come in the evening. Suradasa was very angry. How audacious the priest was, he thought. The Lord of the whole world had blessed him with sight to see all these places and here was an ignorant man denying him darshana!

As the wave of anger rose within him, he was filled with shame. He realised what eyesight had done to him. Throughout his life he had been blind and never felt anger against anyone at all. He saw his Lord with the inner eye in his own mind, and was quite happy. The moment his eyes started seeing, he was filled with desire and anger, and he made demands on others! "How sinful are these eyes!" he thought.

Action Songs

Who Knows

Who knows the white silver mountain?
Who knows the One that dwells on the mountain?

"I know, I know, it is silver Mount Kailasha
Lord Shiva, the great, dwells in Kailasha."

Who knows the white, white bull, wandering on the mountain?
Who knows the angry, angry lion, roaring on the mountain?

"I know, I know, it is Nandi the bull, on whom Lord Shiva rides,
It is Simha the lion, on whom Mother Parvati rides."

Rama, Rama, Rama

I wake up in the morning and say Rama, Rama
Rama Rama Rama Rama Rama Rama Rama
I brush my teeth and say Rama, Rama
Rama Rama Rama Rama RamaRama Rama.

I have my bath and say Rama, Rama
Rama Rama Rama Rama Rama Rama Rama
While eating food I say Rama, Rama
Rama Rama Rama Rama Rama Rama Rama.

I play with friends and say Rama, Rama
Rama Rama Rama Rama Rama Rama Rama.
While sleeping I say Rama, Rama
Rama Rama Rama Rama Rama Rama Rama.

The Play in the Sky

The goddess of the East and the goddess of
the West
Stood up in the morning to play with a red
ball.

The goddess of the East had a rose-pink dress
The goddess of the West had a bluebells dress.

The goddess of the East raised her hand
And threw the ball into the blue blue sky.

The red ball went round and round
The blue, blue sky turned red, red, red.

The goddess of the West had a pink dress now
The goddess of the East had a blue dress now.

When both were tired, the play came to an
end,
They went to bed and the sky was dark.

79

The Temple

Ring-a-ring, Ring-a-ring
The temple bells ring and ring.

I go with mother to worship the Lord
Fruit and flowers we take for Him.

We go to the temple, wash our feet
We go round the temple with folded palms.

We go into the temple and pray to God
We give the fruit and flowers to the Lord.

We touch our eyes when incense is lit
We take Prasada and then go home.

Shabari

Scene One

(*In Dandakaranya Matanga Mahamuni's Ashrama. Shabari, a middle-aged tribal woman, moves about with a worried look*).

Shabari: The time is approaching. My Gurudev will soon be leaving. How can I live alone in the ashrama without my Master? Gurudev, Gurudev, I know nothing, Gurudev. Show me how to live, my Master.

Sage Matanga: (*comes out of the cottage*). Shabari, all is ready. I shall leave in a few minutes. Carry on as usual. You know all that is to be done. Don't be afraid.

Shabari: *(with tears in her eyes)*. Gurudev, I feel lost without your gracious presence. Please permit me to enter the fire and follow you to the other world. Who will look after your needs there, Gurudev?

Matanga: *(with an indulgent smile)*. My child, there I shall not be requiring any of these material things. And that is not a place that you can reach by entering the fire. You have to gain the vision by tapas. Wait here and continue your tapas, as diligently as you are doing now.

Shabari: Gurudev, you have been the object of my meditation, the goal of my services and the centre of my world. With you gone, I am helpless, like a rudderless ship. How am I to live? *(She holds on to his feet and weeps bitterly)*.

Matanga: *(raising her kindly)*. Don't be so worried. Lord Vishnu has taken up an incarnation as Sri Rama in King Dasharatha's house. He is born to kill Ravana and destroy his evil forces, exactly twelve years from now. He and his brother Lakshmana will come to our ashrama in search of Sita, who will have been kidnapped by Ravana. At that time serve the Lord with love. By His darshana you will be released from the bonds of life. It is your privilege to see the Lord in physical form. I shall not be there to see Him because this body's work is over. Now let me leave.

Shabari: *(entreating him).* Not yet, Gurudev, please remain for a while and instruct me how to conduct myself during the twelve years until the Lord comes.

Matanga: Prepare yourself to receive the Lord with complete devotion. Spend your time fully in the contemplation and remembrance of the Lord. When the Lord comes, not only you, but every bird, rabbit, squirrel, tree and plant, nay, the whole ashrama should welcome Him. Train all these children of yours how to love the Lord and welcome Him.

Shabari: Gurudev, I don't even know what the Lord looks like or what He does. How shall I meditate on Him? What does He look like?

Matanga: Close your eyes and behold His beautiful earthly form, His leela here!

Shabari: (*Closes her eyes. Displays ecstasy, joy, wonderment and contentment at the vision within*). Oh, Gurudev!

Matanga: This is the wonderful form in which the Lord will come to you. In these twelve years do tapas, constantly contemplate on this form and await His arrival. The Lord at that time will be very sad because of separation from His beloved Sita. Comfort Him and serve Him. Immediately thereafter, you will attain moksha.

Shabari: Gurudev, please leave me some token of your presence here by which I can find some consolation.

Matanga: All right. Those wet clothes on that stone there. Don't wash them, but let them remain there. For twelve years until it is time for you to leave, they will remain fresh and wet as they are now. (*Shabari smiles happily. As she prostrates, the sage blesses her and sits in meditation to let go of his body*).

(*The curtain falls*).

Scene Two

(*Same setting. Shabari is working around the ashrama. Her lips are constantly uttering the name of the Lord*).

Shabari: (*sweeping*). Srirama, Srirama, Srirama, Srirama, Srirama (*many tribal children come running from all directions. She looks at them with affection*). Ah, you have come, my dears! Come and sit here. I shall tell you all about my Rama. Sing along with me.(*She sits down and the children sit around her*).

Srirama Srirama Srirama Jayarama, Srirama Srirama Srirama Jayarama Srirama Rama Jaya Rama Rama Rama.

(*All the children joyously sing along with her. Even the trees appear to sing. Two parrots sitting on the tree are very attentive*).

(Parrots repeat). Srirama Srirama, Srirama, Srirama, Srirama *(All the children look at them in surprise).*

(The curtain falls and rises again).

(There are more children around Shabari. On the branches of the trees are parrots, cuckoos, mynahs and nightingales, eager to sing. As the curtain rises, they chant, Srirama Rama Rama, Jayrama Rama).

Shabari: Do you know, my dears, how my Lord takes avatara on earth as a man? When there is

too much of sin in the world, when the good people suffer, then Mother Earth prays to the Lord. Gods and sages also pray to the Lord. Then He is born on earth. Now the Lord is born as Srirama.

One child: Ma, where is the Lord born?

Shabari: In Ayodhya, dear. He is born as the eldest son of King Dasharatha.

Another child: Ma, why was the Lord born there? Had He been born here, we would have played with Him.

Shabari: *(sighing)*. How nice it would have been! But, my dear, only great souls have such a privilege. Do you know how long the king had to do austerities to get the Lord as his son! King Dasharatha had three wives, Kaushalya, Sumitra and Kaikeyi. For a long time he had no children. Then he performed a big sacrifice. A divine being came out of the fire and gave him some payasam. The king divided that payasam into two portions and gave one to Kaushalya and the other to Kaikeyi. They divided their shares into

87

two and gave one each to Sumitra. They all drank the payasam. My Lord Rama was born to Kaushalya, Lakshmana and Shatrughana to Sumitra and Bharata to Kaikeyi.

One child: Ma, why will the Lord come here?

Shabari: My child, the Lord marries His divine consort Lakshmi, who is born as Sita in the house of King Janaka. When King Dasharatha wants to crown my Lord as the King, Kaikeyi comes in the way by asking for two boons. She wants her son Bharata to be made the king and Rama to be sent to the forest for fourteen years.

Another child: Why does Kaikeyi ask for such a thing? Isn't she cruel?

Shabari: Yes, my child, she is cruel. Yet, she is not. It is kindness to us. If Rama remains in Ayodhya, how can we see Him? He is coming here to give us His darshana, my dears. Lakshmana will also be with Him.

Another child: Ma, where is Sita now?

Shabari: Who knows, my child? *(with tears in her eyes)*. My Lord is delicate, like a flower. How His feet will be aching with the rough path here! There are fierce animals in these forests. How much they will trouble Him!

Another child: Ma, if He comes here we will wash His feet. We will remove the thorns from His feet.

Another child: Ma, if I am with Him, I shall pick up all the stones and the thorns from the path, so that they can't hurt Him while He is walking.

Another child: Ma, I will teach the tigers and the lions how to sing 'Srirama Srirama' and to love Him, and not to harm our Lord.

Shabari: *(smiling cheerfully)*. Yes, yes, my children, go to all corners of our forest and tell everyone that the Lord will be coming within three years. Teach the tigers and the lions, the cobras and the serpents, the bears and the boars. Teach them how to sing of the Lord. Pick up all the stones and make all the paths in our forests better. Teach my Lord's name to the trees and plants and make them blossom sweetly. Sing, my children.

Srirama, Srirama, Srirama, Jayarama
Srirama, Srirama, Srirama, Jayarama.
(The children, the birds and the trees repeat the Lord's name in unison as Shabari chants it in soft, loving tones).

(The curtain falls).

Scene Three

(The same scene. The whole ashrama is bedecked with flowers. The trees are in full bloom, on their top branches are birds of all kinds, while on the lower branches are monkeys. On one side various animals shelter under the shade of trees while on the other, the children stand with flowers in their hands. The central stone, which is to be the seat of Sri Rama, is finely decorated. On the side are heaps of ripe fruit of various kinds. The whole ashrama resounds with singing "Srirama Rama Rama, Jaya Rama Rama").

Shabari: *(doing the final check that everything is ready and proper).* "Srirama Rama Rama Jaya

Rama Rama Rama". My Lord must have reached the forest by now. How tired He must be! My Rama, how much trouble You have to undergo for our sake! "Srirama Rama Rama Jaya Rama Rama Rama". O Rama, I am an ignorant woman. Will my service be to Your taste? My poor Lord, are You separated from Your divine consort? Can I see Your sorrowful face? How I wish that I could bring Mother Sita and present her to You! "Sri Rama Rama Rama, Jaya Rama Rama Rama".

(From one side Sri Rama and Lakshmana enter. The joyous cries of "Srirama Jayarama" fill the air, as the animals, birds and children hail Sri Rama and shower flowers on Him. Shabari rushes forward and leads the brothers forward towards the stone seat. Sri Rama sits on the stone while Lakshmana stands behind Him. Shabari washes Sri Rama's feet and hands and one child offers water to Lakshmana. Then she garlands Rama and sits near Him with folded palms).

Shabari: *(shedding tears of joy).* My Lord, how long I have waited for this day! Ever since my Gurudev showed me Your Divine form, day in and day out I have been seeing You. Look, the whole forest has been eagerly waiting for Your darshana.

Sri Rama: *(looks around with affection).* Blessed are you, Mother! With your devotion you have converted the whole forest into an ashrama. Tell me more about your venerable Guru Matanga Mahamuni.

Shabari: My Gurudev ascended to the Supreme twelve years ago, Rama. That day he told me that You would be coming here. He told me that on seeing You my tapas would be over. Blessed are my eyes that behold You thus. Blessed are my ears for hearing Your voice. How I have waited for the dawn of this day! My dear children wish to welcome You with a song. May they, O Lord?

Sri Rama: Mother, I am eager to listen to them.

Shabari: *(in ecstatic love, leads).*
Srirama Rama Jaya Rama, Sringara Rama Raghurama
Karunya Rama Raghurama, Kodandarama Jaya Rama.

(As Shabari stops, first the children, then the birds, then the animals and last of all the monkeys sing and repeat the kirtana).

Kalyana Rama Srirama, Kamaniya Rama Jaya Rama
Atmabhirama Srirama, Seetabhirama Srirama.

(They repeat the song in the same manner. Sri Rama and Lakshmana look on with wonder at how perfectly and melodiously the animals and the birds repeat the song).

Sri Rama: *(embracing Shabari with love).* Shabari, even the stones and the brooks burst with devotion, what wonder if the birds and animals do so?

Shabari: *(overjoyed)* The whole world adores You, my Lord, what to say of us, the ignorant? My Rama, You must be hungry after Your long walk this morning. *(She brings a leaf with fruits and places it in front of Sri Rama. Then she gives another leaf with fruits to Lakshmana. Sri Rama takes up one fruit to put in His mouth).*

Shabari: *(in agony)* Ah! My Rama, don't eat that. It doesn't look sweet enough. Let me see. *(She takes the fruit from Sri Rama's hand and tastes it. She nods in satisfaction and hands the fruit back to Him).* Yes, it is sweet. You will like it. *(One by one she tastes the fruits and gives them to Him. With a smile He takes them and eats with relish).*

(The shouts of Srirama Jayarama reach the sky).

The curtain comes down.

CODE OF CONDUCT FOR
THE CHINMAYA MISSION MEMBERS

Chinmaya Mission members should:

- Try to live up to and fulfill the motto as well as the pledge of the Mission.

- Daily spare time for meditation and scriptural study.

- Once a week, on a convenient day offer prayers at a nearby temple with members of their family.

- Discover a life of harmony at home and on no account create any domestic unhappiness.

- Have satsanga at home with the children and other family members. Reading of the Ramayana, Mahabharata and Bhagavata Mahapurana in a language familiar to the children would be an important part of the programme.

- Greet other Mission members with 'Hari Om'.

- Inculcate the practice of daily offering pranamas to the elders in the house.

THE CHINMAYA MISSION PLEDGE

We stand as one family
bound to each other with love and respect.

We serve as an army
courageous and disciplined,
ever ready to fight against
all low tendencies and false values,
within and without us.

We live honestly
the noble life of sacrifice and service,
producing more than what we consume,
and giving more than what we take.

We seek the Lord's grace
to keep us on the path of virtue, courage and
wisdom.

May Thy grace and blessings
flow through us to the world around us.

We believe that the service of our country
is the service of the Lord of Lords,
and devotion to the people
is the devotion to the supreme Self.

We know our responsibilities,
give us the ability and courage
to fulfil them.

Om Tat Sat